ENGAGING YOUTH

Engaging

Combating the Youth

Apathy of Young Americans
toward Politics

Kevin Mattson

A CENTURY FOUNDATION REPORT

The Century Foundation Press   •   New York

The Century Foundation sponsors and supervises timely analyses of economic policy, foreign affairs, and domestic political issues. Not-for-profit and nonpartisan, it was founded in 1919 and endowed by Edward A. Filene.

LIBRARY OF CONGRESS CATALOGING-IN-PUBLICATION DATA

Mattson, Kevin, 1966-
    Engaging youth: combating the apathy of young Americans toward politics / Kevin Mattson.
        p.   cm.
"A Century Foundation report."
Includes bibliographical references (p. 55) and index.
    ISBN 0-87078-470-6
    1.   Youth--United States--Political activity. 2.   Political alienation--United States. 3.   Political culture--United States.   I. Title.
    HQ799.2.P6 M38 2003
    305.235'0973--dc21

                                                                    2003013716

Cover design and illustration/graphics by Claude V. Goodwin.
Manufactured in the United States of America.

FOREWORD

Historians are cautious when it comes to predicting how any particular generation of young people will turn out in the long run. But there is reason to believe, based on historical experience, that no generation will be given the equivalent of a free ride. That is, each new cohort of young people, in the fullness of time, will confront its own challenges. The way such tests are met counts heavily in the eventual summing up of how such a generation performed and how they are remembered.

Popular culture, however, is not willing to wait for the test of time, often descending to a relatively crude and inevitably oversimplified characterization of a generation. One manifestation of this inclination on the part of pop culture pundits is the acute desire to find a nickname that seems particularly apt for describing a group of diverse individuals who live through a common era. Thus, those Americans who faced the challenges of the Great Depression and of World War II (now most often called the "greatest generation") sometimes have been referred to as the "civic generation." And the very large number of citizens born during the period from 1946 to 1964 have long been branded the "baby boomers," although this reference to their numbers conveys little information about the role they played in many transformations, particularly during the 1960s.

Of course, the civic generation, in important respects, was coerced into its engagement with great public questions and historic changes. No one chooses to live through terrible economic crises or even more terrible global warfare as a personal preference. Still, how civics coped with these catastrophes affected both the development of the nation and the reputation of the generation itself in profound ways. The ambitious programs of the Roosevelt revolution, for example, helped

v

to shape their view of what government could and should do. The war intensified the sense that public entities could and must play a major role in dealing with life's challenges. When millions of young men were drafted into the armed services (about 15 million served at a time when the population was only 120 million), the country changed whether it chose to or not. In other words, what happened was in response to depression and war rather than a voluntary intellectual awakening or a commitment to a particular set of ideas about the public agenda and how such ideas could be critical to their lives. Then during the 1950s, when peace and prosperity provided the freedom to ignore such questions, these same Americans became known as the "passive generation."

Indeed, after the apparent complacency of the 1950s, the activism of later decades was certain to define the experience of a new group of Americans reaching adulthood and joining the workforce: the boomer generation. Boomers came of age just when enormous changes in society and culture were reaching critical mass. The ideas of the sexual revolution, women's liberation, and especially civil rights were hardly new, but they achieved an immense enhancement both in terms of popular support and media attention during the 1960s. The sharp differences in circumstances between Vietnam and World War II intensified the sense that all had changed—and that the boomers were in some way largely responsible for the new American political and cultural landscape. In fact, many of those changes sprang from the leadership of activists from an older generation, including Martin Luther King, Jr., Michael Harrington, and Betty Friedan.

So perhaps it is not surprising that, in recent years, scholars and popular observers have struggled to make sense of the young Americans who followed the now-aging boomers. The task of characterizing them successfully is not easy. And the question of what they will do to reshape the nation is yet to be determined.

In this report, Kevin Mattson focuses on the extent to which the current generation of young adults appears to be uninterested in public affairs and cynical about government and politics. One of the more interesting forces he examines is the extensive infrastructure that conservative institutions have developed to influence young minds. One of Mattson's primary examples of how this works is the case of proposals to privatize Social Security. He reveals how those groups have tried to characterize privatization as a generational issue, explaining the extent to which they have seized on the inevitable differences in the way the world looks to young people as opposed to the way it looks to their elders who have a more realistic sense of their own financial prospects and therefore of their economic vulnerability. The truth is that, in their sales pitches to the young, these groups overlook the fact that diverting a portion of payroll taxes from the Social Security system in order to fund private accounts for young people could only be accomplished by reducing payments to future retirees.

In this era of antigovernment sentiment, it is probably not surprising that right-wing advocacy groups and think tanks would challenge the notion that the public sector can do a good, efficient, and reliable job of providing a floor to support retirement for the elderly, even in the face of the overwhelming evidence that the government has, in fact, for more than sixty years, operated with negligible overhead the largest retirement and survivor's insurance programs in the world, achieving dramatic success in reducing poverty among the elderly.

Mattson's conclusion is important: in the face of the civic apathy of so many young people, the current passivity of both our progressive political leaders and the country in general is not acceptable. This work should stimulate more research and writing about the need for and content of progressive engagement of this generation of Americans. Like their predecessors, they are sure to face problems and opportunities. How they address such questions will help shape the American future. We thank Kevin Mattson for this exploration of some of the vital issues concerning that process.

RICHARD C. LEONE, *President*
The Century Foundation
January 2003

CONTENTS

ACKNOWLEDGMENTS

My first thanks go to Ruy Teixeira of The Century Foundation. He worked with me to turn an idea into an actual project. Thanks also to the other Century Foundation readers who helped sharpen my arguments and to Sarah Ritchie at The Century Foundation, who organized a roundtable that addressed the issues that I write about here. For research help, I thank Gokhan Balaban, who did numerous interviews with students at Rutgers University about their political attitudes. The Whitman Center at Rutgers University, where I worked for six years before coming to Ohio University, has supported me in all my endeavors. Thanks especially to Benjamin Barber, the director of the Whitman Center.

Chapter 1

Introduction:

A New Lost Generation?

E ver since the baby boom generation—those who were born in the
wake of World War II and came of age during the 1960s—won its
label, pundits and marketers have been searching for a new tag line
for the next generation, those born during and after the 1960s. For a
while, members of this generation were thought to be spoiled and
withdrawn and were thus labeled "slackers." Then came the blasé
but less offensive "twentysomethings"; then the term that stuck,
"Generation X" (coined in Douglas Coupland's novel about young
adults frightened of commitment and working low-paying, service
sector "McJobs"). Then we heard that this Generation X (and those
a bit younger now known as Generation Y) was actually hardworking,
pragmatic, even entrepreneurial, certainly ready for a "new economy."
Young people were the computer-savvy "netizens" who would lead us
into the utopia of the 1990s economic bubble. In all of this generational
labeling—much of it invented by corporate marketers interested
in niche advertising—one characteristic has seemed to stick: political
apathy. If we take traditional forms of political participation—
especially voting but also informing oneself about public affairs—
Generation X and Y come up short.

In 1971, the Twenty-sixth Amendment lowered the voting age to
eighteen. The first generation to benefit from this change votes in
record low numbers. Elizabeth Hubbard of the Pew Foundation
recently noted, "Over the last twenty years, the decline in voter
turnout has been most apparent among young adults."[1] In 1994, for

1

instance, one in five eligible young voters (meaning those registered, hence not all young people) showed up for midterm elections.[2] Recent estimates put the youth vote (eighteen- to twenty-nine-year-olds) in the 2000 presidential election at about 38 percent.[3] When asked about their political knowledge, young adults seem out of the loop. In a poll of college freshmen, only 26 percent said "keeping up to date with political affairs" was important.[4] As political scientist Robert Putnam recently summed it up, members of Generation X, in comparison with those who came of age during World War II (the "civic generation") and baby boomers, are "less interested in politics, less informed about current events (except for scandal, personality, and sports), less likely to attend a public meeting, less likely to contact public officials, less likely to attend church, less likely to work with others on some community project, and less likely to contribute financially to a church or charity or political cause."[5] Generation X now seems better labeled Generation Apathetic.

Some political, academic, and philanthropic leaders rank this youthful apathy as a fundamental problem. John McCain, for instance, took note of young people's cynicism about government. He warned during his primary campaign that "we must reform the way the campaigns are financed in America today to restore the confidence of these young people in the institutions of government."[6] Major foundations—including the Carnegie Corporation of New York, the Pew Charitable Trusts, the Ford Foundation, the Kellogg Foundation, and The Century Foundation—have programs directed at reengaging young people in political activity. Numerous colleges are experimenting with community service programs that educate young people in civic responsibility. Young people's political disaffection now appears to constitute a major American problem—and for obvious reasons.

Although saying so seems like a cliché, young people are America's future. If they are increasingly apathetic about public life, public life will continue to deplete itself. Indeed, in a recent national poll more than two out of three eighteen- to thirty-four-year-olds expressed detachment from their government.[7] This correlates with what Ruy Teixeira calls "an astonishing increase in political cynicism over the last several decades."[8] It is hard to imagine democracy operating in a healthy fashion with the levels of public mistrust among young people today. Government will increasingly find it difficult to justify its role in society. Youth apathy—especially if it continues to grow or even just holds steady—should trouble us.

With this in mind, though, it is important not to work ourselves into a collective lather or fall prey to hand-wringing laments about apathetic youth. I am wary of those from the right or left who claim that youth apathy about politics should lead us to overthrow our present political institutions. Rather, we should try to understand what youth apathy tells us about contemporary politics. Take the act of voting, for instance. Certainly, younger adults have shown higher levels of disengagement than other adults, and since World War II, young people have *always* been less likely to vote than other groups of citizens.[9] And even though voter decline is still happening across the board in America, the decline among young people is greater than that of all voters.

As two leading political scientists point out, "In general, as people grow older, their involvement in politics deepens."[10] Young people are in a phase of life less conducive to political and civic participation; they are busy moving around and finding work, not yet settled down. Thus, many political scientists counsel relaxation about Generation X's civic disaffection. After an in-depth exploration of research on Generation X and politics (much of it quite gloomy), two political scientists stated, "It is likely that X'ers will eventually find their political voice(s) and take their place, naturally enough, at the table of power."[11] As can be seen in Figure 1.1 (see page 4), Generation X'ers seemed to turn out in fairly larger numbers during Bill Clinton's first election—perhaps drawn to some of the more idealistic sentiments expressed in 1992 (plus concern about a sinking economy). The recent upswing in youth activism, witnessed in the anti-sweatshop movement on America's college campuses, should alleviate some of our concerns about Generation X's and Generation Y's apathy. And who knows what the recent terrorist attacks on America will bring in terms of changed perceptions among young people of government and public life?[12]

With all of this said, though, there does seem something quite different about Generation X. If anything, this generation seems to be *leading* other Americans in terms of an overall civic decline. Robert Putnam has gained much fame recently for warning that Americans are too often "bowling alone" and not joining local civic groups as they did in the past. Putnam's work is a provocative mix of social science and moral jeremiad. He worries quite a bit about Generation X but then celebrates the increasing hours of Generation X's voluntary and public service. He expresses exuberance about the "commitment to volunteerism" that he sees among young people today. In fact, he goes

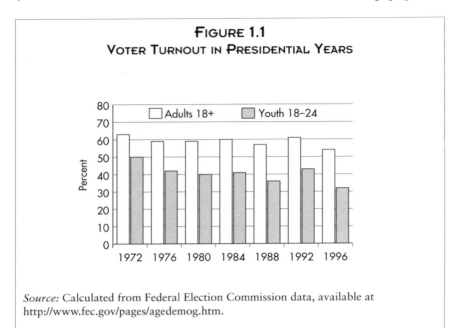

FIGURE 1.1
VOTER TURNOUT IN PRESIDENTIAL YEARS

Source: Calculated from Federal Election Commission data, available at
http://www.fec.gov/pages/agedemog.htm.

on to say, "This development is the most promising sign that America
might be on the cusp of a new period of civic renewal, especially if this
youthful volunteerism persists into adulthood and begins to expand
beyond individual caregiving to broader engagement with social and
political issues."[13] Here we come to the crux of the matter and to one
of the central arguments of this report. In fact, volunteerism is *not*
increasing more traditional forms of political engagement—voting,
educating oneself about political issues, helping out on a campaign,
contributing time and money to a political organization.[14] Indeed,
young people's rising levels of volunteerism are accompanied by continued political apathy. The idea that the public sector should play
any role in our collective lives seems to be coming to an end.

Generation X is not composed only of libertarian conservatives
(those who reject government out and out), for there are certainly
younger progressives active today. This generation *has* been deeply
influenced, however, by a rightward shift in American politics,
captured in Ronald Reagan's famous quip that "government is not
the solution but the problem." Even those who might be expected
to have more idealistic views of government than Reagan did—

especially those engaged in public and voluntary service—wind up showing distrust of government and the public sector. They characterize their personal acts of "doing good" as something above politics. At the same time, Generation X has witnessed the growing power of money in politics, an influence that further diminishes any idealism about political activism or hope in government (and one reason why McCain has been right to target youth disaffection as a major impetus to reforming campaign finance). We need to do something about campaign financing before we chastise young people for staying away from traditional politics. The renewal of progressivism and the cleaning up of American politics are inherently tied, in my opinion, to a need to reengage a generation that appears increasingly apathetic.

The emphasis on the progressive response to this problem is critical to my argument. While many bemoan a *general* civic crisis in America, I see a much greater crisis for progressive and liberal ideals. Since the rise of Barry Goldwater, conservative political philosophy has articulated distrust if not contempt of government. Today's distrust of government and the public sector is thus more damaging to progressives, who put much more faith in that sector. In keeping with Reagan's quip about government being the problem, numerous political leaders such as Phil Gramm and Dick Armey have attacked the federal government. Even a supposedly more centrist Republican such as George W. Bush complains that tax dollars are not the government's money—arguing against the whole premise of collective and public goods. In fact, many conservative organizations and pundits have done much to inflame youth dissatisfaction with government and public life. Conservatives might well bemoan the fact that young people do not vote, but they are probably less concerned with expressions of distrust in public life more generally. I suspect that political scientists, such as Robert Putnam, who have discovered a general civic crisis have not paid enough attention to the *political* dimensions of the problem.

This report begins by explaining how youth political disengagement fits into American history and political culture. The political beliefs of Generation X may not be easy to label (after all, class, race, and gender often determine beliefs more than age), but we can at least get a better handle on the *political world* within which many of its members (this author included) grew up. As with so much else, we need to go back to the 1960s to find some explanations of why young people might not be as active today as were their predecessors in the 1960s. Then we can analyze how pundits and other spokespeople have tried to interpret Generation X's existing political attitudes to support certain political conclusions and agendas that have an increasingly anti-government and right-wing leaning. Based on certain reported activities (including declines in voter participation and increases in voluntary service, for instance), conflicting conceptions of young people and politics have emerged. Much of this debate about Generation X's political beliefs seems shoddy. I offer here some of my own, albeit limited, proposals for counteracting young people's political apathy and rebuilding a more public-minded vision of politics.

Chapter 2

THE LEGACY OF THE 1960S

Whenever people discuss the apathy of Generation X, they quickly realize that hovering in the background is a "golden age" when young people supposedly participated in American politics in record numbers—namely the 1960s. The protest movements of that time as well as the rise of the New Left and a "counterculture" represent an idealism that many critics believe is missing today. Not surprisingly, those who were young in this remarkable period of American history are often the same ones complaining about the civic apathy of Generation X. At the same time, Generation X'ers have learned to roll their eyes as their baby boomer elders talk about the "good old days." As one young author put it, Generation X'ers often feel that they are living "in the shadow of the sixties."[1]

The reasons young people became so strongly associated with political idealism and activism in the 1960s are numerous. Key among them was the rise of a "youth culture," which some historians date back to the 1920s but most see coming to fruition during the 1950s. As middle-class young people no longer went to work at early ages, they experienced what some call a postponed adolescence. The number of middle-class youth entering higher education institutions skyrocketed during the 1950s and 1960s, as did the post–World War II affluence (witnessed in increased incomes, suburban homes, and automobiles). It is no wonder that many of the key New Left issues grew out of academia—the "free speech" movement, protests against universities' collusion with the military, the "teach-in" movement. There were other peculiar historical circumstances of the 1950s and 1960s that generated the civil rights movement. There was a heightening of the cold war, along with the Vietnam War and the protests against it. Young people became leaders in many of the political movements of the time. Out of this, the idea that "youth will make the revolution"— to quote one of many overblown 1960s slogans—blossomed. But this heightened youth activism owed as much to the politics of the time as to any exceptional amount of idealism in one particular generation. In retrospect, the New Left left behind few institutions capable of outlasting the 1960s. As the historian Alan Brinkley has argued persuasively: "The new radicals never developed the organizational or institutional skills necessary for building an enduring movement."[2] After all, the two major organizations of student activists—Students for a Democratic Society (SDS) and the Student Non-Violent Coordinating Committee (SNCC)—fell apart by the late 1960s. If anything, the longest-lasting legacy of these organizations is a split between student activism and electoral politics that continues today.

Even before the collapse of SDS and SNCC, there arose a form of what I will call *anti-politics* among some young leaders within the civil rights movement. The 1964 compromise over the Mississippi Freedom Democratic Party turned off many SNCC members from working within the seemingly compromised world of electoral politics. Organizers within the civil rights movement had tried to seat themselves as Mississippi's delegates to the Democratic Party convention (this was when conventions were still quite spontaneous, not the rehearsed, televised spectacles they are today, even if they were controlled by party bosses). The leaders of the Democratic Party, working with President Lyndon Baines Johnson, came back with a compromise that insulted many of SNCC's members. Martin Luther King, Jr., saw the compromise as morally contestable but felt that SNCC must nevertheless accept it. Robert Moses, a young activist within SNCC, went one step further. As historian Taylor Branch points out, Moses saw the compromise as "a bitter turning point . . . for all of American politics," and he argued that "we're not here to bring politics to our morality but to bring morality to our politics."[3] Moses wanted activism to be divorced from the inherently corrupt and compromised world of electoral politics. He did not give up on activism—in fact, he argued for organizing Freedom Schools and (perhaps ironically) voter registration drives throughout the South— but he saw activism as distinct from traditional politics. The argument had a long-lasting impact on youth activism.

   Other activists such as Allard Lowenstein and intellectuals such
as Arnold Kaufman, by contrast, tried to keep young people within
the Democratic Party and active within electoral politics during the
1960s.[4] As we know from the histories told by Todd Gitlin and James
Miller, SDS and SNCC became enamored with ideas of revolution
and guerrilla warfare rather than long-term political struggle within
representative institutions.[5] As SNCC turned to "black power" and
the idea of revolution, its membership drifted away from the
grassroots organizing that Robert Moses had counseled.[6] Thus,
Lowenstein's and Kaufman's arguments fell on deaf ears, and there
can be little doubt that the demise of SNCC and SDS left behind
not simply a lack of institutions on the left but also the legacy of anti-
politics on the progressive side of the political spectrum in America.
   Along with this anti-politics, the most important and durable
legacy of the 1960s came from the right. Barry Goldwater might have
run a disastrous campaign in 1964, but American political discourse
today is framed much more by Goldwater libertarianism than by the
left-leaning, participatory democratic, and welfare statist arguments
found in SDS's Port Huron Statement, the founding document of the
New Left written in 1962. Ronald Reagan learned a great deal from
his participation in the Goldwater campaign. Young Americans for
Freedom—the youth wing of the American right—was instrumental
in Goldwater's run and is still quite active today (it picked up steam,
not surprisingly, during the Reagan administration). Conservative
intellectuals outlasted Goldwater and have grown in power ever since
the 1960s. Young historians such as Rick Perlstein have recognized
that the real victor in American politics, from the 1960s onward, was
the right.[7]
   Unlike certain portions of the left, the right never gave up on
electoral politics. William Buckley, conservative intellectual and edi-
tor of *National Review*, called on a group of Goldwater supporters in
1964 to "infuse the conservative spirit in enough people to entitle us
to look about us . . . not at the ashes of defeat," which Buckley knew
was to come for Goldwater that year, "but at the well planted seeds
of hope, which will flower on a great November day in the future."[8]
Buckley understood that the right could eventually triumph if it transformed American thinking (through publications such as his own
magazine and those produced by think tanks) while also getting politicians into office. The history of the 1980s and 1990s attests to
Buckley's foresight.

   The eventual strength of the right and the limited accomplish-
ments of the left have led some historians to downplay 1960s idealism. Historians such as Perlstein make clear that the victories of the
right overshadow those of the left. Kenneth Heineman has gone one
step further. In his book on student revolt during the 1960s,
Heineman points out correctly that the majority of "youths who
joined SDS came from upper-middle-class households," while only
"17 percent of SDSers could claim blue-collar origins."9 Highlighting
"the importance of class in the 1960s student protest," Heineman
argues that "for upper-middle-class white youths . . . protest came
cost-free, while the poor died in the Vietnam War."10 This is not an
entirely new idea, of course; political leaders such as Richard Nixon
and George Wallace made similar points at the height of conflict. But
Heineman is a historian, not a political leader looking for ways to
attract voters. He seems to suggest that we must rework our entire
narrative about the 1960s, ditching tales of bold and courageous protesters in favor of understanding protest as privilege.
   Heineman is right on one very important point: the leaders of the
1960s protest movements came largely from positions of privilege.
Nonetheless, I think a responsible left had emerged prior to the anti-
politics of SNCC and the revolutionary high jinks of late 1960s SDS.
The political philosophy of "radical liberalism" espoused by Arnold
Kaufman and Allard Lowenstein captured the potential of this 1960s
radicalism. As I have shown in my book *Intellectuals in Action*, the
original New Left was based largely on a desire to fuse a sense of
social justice with the concept of participatory democracy (best represented in new social movements).11 The original proponents of the
Port Huron Statement tried to balance the sort of community-based
participation they saw operating in the civil rights movement with a
strong federal government capable of helping those most in need.
This is the sort of vision that is desperately needed today, with, of
course, requisite reworking for our changed circumstances (as will
become clearer later in this report). Unfortunately, the right has done
much to drive this vision off the table of political discussion. It is most
important to understand why middle-class young people might not
be drawn to this sort of idealism or long-term political struggle—that
is, why those from positions of privilege, those who have the time
and comfort, seem to be less attracted to political idealism.
   Here I agree with Heineman but take his argument in a different
direction. Middle-class people have taken a lead in struggles for social

justice. After all, they have the capacity (or privilege, if the term is preferred) to work on things beyond the immediate pressures of work and family. Their basic needs are taken care of, so they can engage in less "practical" projects. This report, therefore, will focus on the worlds of middle- and upper-middle-class youth—obviously a limited perspective—and will leave out numerous working-class and poor young people (many of them new immigrants) who have drastically changed the face of young America since the 1960s. Nonetheless, to understand the recent divide between young people and political participation, and their disaffection from progressive politics more particularly, it becomes necessary to focus on those who have the *option* of becoming engaged in politics. What has happened to the world of middle- and upper-middle-class youth since the 1960s that helps explain their disaffection from politics and public life more broadly? Additionally, how has the residue of anti-politics from the 1960s affected them? There are historical reasons for political apathy. In addition, some have deployed apathy to create a self-serving agenda. We need to understand both what these historical reasons are and how they have served as fertile ground for the right.

Chapter 3

HISTORICAL REASONS FOR THE DECLINE?
CHANGES IN AMERICAN POLITICAL CULTURE

THE COMPLICATIONS OF POLITICS SINCE THE 1960S

Despite the arguments of Heineman and neoconservatives, many people still view the 1960s as a golden age of youthful liberalism and activism. Indeed, the progressive and leftist activists interviewed for this project said they felt bereft of "big causes."[1] There seems no distinct generational experience that liberal or progressive young people can rally around. As the *Washington Post* recently reported, "The protesters of the 21st century do not have a single galvanizing aim, such as ending the war in Vietnam. . . . Today's causes are more nebulous, more nuanced than the issues of years past. . . ."[2] In fact, many young activists not only lack the big causes of the past but also seem to struggle with the consequences and complicated inheritances from the protest movements of the 1960s.

Take for instance the women's movement of the 1960s–1970s. Its leaders based many of their principles and activities on arguments found in books such as Betty Friedan's *The Feminine*

Mystique. Friedan argued that women suffered from a lack of choice. Their horizons were limited by a "comfortable concentration camp," the term she provocatively used to describe the 1950s household. Friedan was ambivalent about what would happen if women pursued careers in the corporate world; nonetheless, she clearly thought that purposeful work was the most important goal for women to accomplish if they were to become equal to men. Fighting for inclusion in the workplace seemed the paramount task ahead for women.

Although the Equal Rights Amendment was never passed, it is clear that many young, middle-class women (the sort Friedan addressed) pursue careers today without the sort of barriers they would have faced in the 1960s. This is not to say that there is no longer any sex discrimination. But there seems less demand for a movement uniting young women around inclusion. Today's struggles are adjudicated through the legal system, not in the streets. Young women now face issues that are slightly more complex and nuanced than simply demanding equity. A new set of problems center on the consequences of women entering the workforce: everyday forms of condescension in the workplace (not just sexual harassment), the stresses of the two-income family, the difficulty of finding decent child care, the challenges of family leave, and the like. Young women today are trying to live with dignity as new opportunities have opened up for them. Jennifer Baumgardner and Amy Richards proclaim that "young women today feel as if they live their feminist lives without clear political struggles." They are "living self-determined lives" but are no longer "radicals on the ramparts."[3] Feminism is not dead, but its rallying cry has been toned down. (Of course, it may open up again around issues such as abortion.)

Think also of the civil rights movement. During the late 1950s and early 1960s, there were certainly debates about protest techniques, but the cause seemed relatively clear cut: full inclusion and equality for African-Americans. Much of the inspiration for the New Left grew out of this idealistic struggle. But once whites were expelled from SNCC in 1965, things started to change. With the rise of "black power," inclusion came into question. This idea has morphed into contemporary identity politics, which provokes no sense of unity on the left, only debate. Debates also surround race-based affirmative action, with some arguing for more class-based affirmative action. Those organizations that still focus on racial inclusion and political equality—most famously the NAACP—are finding it harder to attract young people.⁴ The original, clear-cut political vision of a Martin Luther King, Jr., has been complicated by changed historical circumstances.

Another way to see the general breakdown of 1960s protest is in the way young people react to stories told about the counterculture. Beats and hippies found an easy target to rebel against in the stuffy and supposedly hypocritical world of their suburban parents— the "organization men" and repressed housewives of the 1950s. Cultural rebellion seemed straightforward: personal liberation, whatever form it took, confronted the shackles of repression. But for many social critics today, the counterculture seems to have become easily incorporated into our hyped-up consumer culture. Critics such as Tom Frank argue that, instead of being idealists, the hippies from the past seem more like the rearguard of larger changes within consumer capitalism. After all, advertising now hypes the idea of rebellion and makes fun of any remnants of cultural conservatism.⁵ For Generation X, the cultural rebellion of the past no longer seems so bold or radical. One of the major reasons that the struggles of the 1960s seem so distant and irrelevant for young people is not only the changed circumstances of politics but also a shift in the American economy. There are no longer too many organization men—those working their entire lives at the same corporation—to rebel against. Indeed, the entire world of work and our conceptions of economic purpose have been transformed since the 1960s. This change explains, if only partially, some of Generation X's changed attitudes about politics.

THE PRESSURES OF THE "NEW ECONOMY" AND NEW FORMS OF WORK

The first and most obvious economic change since the 1950s and 1960s is that more and more young middle-class Americans are working at an earlier age. As Juliet Schor pointed out in her book *The Overworked American*, "Not only are more of the nation's young people working, but they are working longer hours." This is true, as she makes clear, in "suburban America"—that is, among many privileged teens who are not working out of necessity.⁶ They work, undoubtedly, to satisfy their need for disposable income for increased numbers of consumer goods. After all, Generation X is the first to witness advertising even in public schools (with the dawn of Channel One, the corporation that offers television equipment free to public schools while requiring that students watch programming stocked with youth advertising). Someone touting the glories of the so-called new economy, say, a writer such as Daniel Pink, sees only good in what he labels a "flowering of teenage entrepreneurship." Pink boasts, "In San Diego County, 8 percent of high school students already run their own on-line business."[7] What Pink fails to mention is the pile of evidence that young workers find it difficult to stay awake in school and have little time for very much else in life, certainly not participation in or education about politics.[8]

For young adults, business life appeared in a new light during the 1980s and 1990s—especially in comparison to the distrust of business that marked much of the 1960s and 1970s. This changed attitude correlated with an increasing distrust of government. Beginning in the 1970s, as John Judis writes, "The CEOs of large banks and corporations helped to create . . . a powerful network of national organizations, think tanks, trade associations, policy groups, and lobbies." This network espoused a pro-business and anti-regulatory outlook that demonized government and glorified business while countering the "consumer, environmental, and labor movements."[9] By the 1990s, business was reaping the rewards, not only getting more Republicans into office (and pulling the Democrats to the center) but also generating a *pro-business* outlook throughout American culture. The economic boom of the 1990s—a decade that seemed to parallel the 1890s and 1920s—helped cinch the view, even if Americans still expressed major distrust of corporations. With the high-tech explosion, choosing a career in business appeared to be a marvelous act of creativity, even idealism. After all, it was business that was buttressing global awareness and multiculturalism: Cisco Systems advertisements, for instance, showed "a succession of small children from all over the world soberly read[ing] a testimonial to the Internet." In management literature of the time, business leaders appeared as revolutionaries—the source of creativity. "Destruction is cool," bellowed Tom Peters, the leading guru of new managerial theory. As Tom Frank writes, "Benetton was working to equate its brand with the fight against racism, Macintosh with that against technocracy; similarly, Pepsi owned youth rebellion, while Nike staked a claim to 'revolution' generally."[10] Business appeared as a place of idealism and energy. Government did not.

As young people entered the new economy, they discovered that the organization man of the 1950s had long been dead. In his place stood the "free agent" (Daniel Pink's evocative phrase). Temporary, contingent, and part-time labor is quickly becoming the norm throughout today's economy. As Naomi Klein points out, "The use of temp labor in the U.S. has increased by 400 percent since 1982 and that growth has been steady."[11] It goes without saying that part-time labor rarely brings with it benefits such as health insurance (see Table 3.1). Even Pink, who normally says only good things about the new economy's freedom, admits that "about one in three self-employed workers is uninsured" (his numbers are probably low).[12] Nor does the new economy provide any sense of security among workers, let alone loyalty. The result of such economic insecurity shows up in polling done among Generation X workers. As the *Yankelovich Report* put it, "Over two-thirds of Xers agree that, 'I have to take whatever I can get in this world because no one is going to give me anything.' Far fewer Boomers . . . agree."[13] A need to guard one's own self-interest has become primary in America's new economy, especially as the economy becomes the sole source of social provision.

TABLE 3.1
HEALTH INSURANCE FOR TEMP WORKERS (AGE 25–34)

	Total Workers	No Health Plan	Employer Plan	Covered
All Workers	40,718,000	20,160,000	20,559,000	50.5%
Contract	343,000	143,000	200,000	58.3%
Temp	608,000	577,000	31,000	5.1%

Source: Helene Jorgensen, *When Good Jobs Go Bad: Young Adults and Temporary Work in the New Economy* (Washington, D.C.: 2030 Center, 2002), p. 2.

THE CHANGING NATURE OF HIGHER EDUCATION

If the "new economy" teaches self-preservation, it also celebrates education. As we hear over and over, the workforce needs high skill levels that higher educational institutions promise to provide (in this day and age, a high school degree barely gets you noticed in the job market). Interestingly enough, higher levels of education used to be associated with increased political engagement. As Sidney Verba and his colleagues point out, education "enhances nearly every single one of the participatory factors: those who are well-educated have higher incomes and exercise more civic skills; they are more politically interested and informed; they are more likely to be in institutional settings from which they can be recruited into politics." But this magical association between education and political engagement has suddenly disappeared. As Verba explains, "Over the past generation, increasing educational attainment has not been accompanied by parallel increases in political activity. In fact, over the period there has been unambiguous erosion in an important, although atypical, form of participation, voting."[14] This should not be so much of a surprise.

During the 1960s, most students who took part in protest movements and politics "majored in liberal arts and the social sciences."[15] No direct correlation can be shown between these majors and political engagement, but it is likely that these areas of study helped open up larger questions about society and politics that enhanced political engagement. Since the 1960s, and during the time of precipitous decline in political participation that Sidney Verba notes, the number of students in the humanities and social sciences has plummeted. The decline has sharpened most recently. As Russell Jacoby writes, "In the last fifteen years traditional majors such as philosophy, history, and English have declined, while business and management majors have doubled."[16] From 1970 to 1994, the number of bachelor's degrees in computer and information sciences also grew five- to ten-fold.[17] In bolting from the humanities, young people have simply reflected the values they have received from their culture at large. The messages to be economically practical come from everywhere today. Jacoby tells the story of a bank that rejected students' credit card applications when they "listed majors in the humanities, such as English, history or art."[18] The message to abandon humanistic studies for business majors has only been accentuated by the 1990s economic boom.

To add insult to injury, tuition rates at most universities have skyrocketed since the 1980s. In 1980, income from tuition and fees for "degree-granting institutions" stood at $13,773,259; by 1996, the number had risen to $55,260,293.[19] Student loan debt has risen right alongside tuition. During the first half of the year 2000 alone, student debt has risen 3.5 percent (see Table 3.2), and it shows no sign of stopping.[20] With this increase, young people have a harder time considering a career in the nonprofit realm or in politics when they come out of college or graduate school. Business and subsidiary fields such as corporate law carry the biggest appeal, precisely because they promise big incomes that can pay off increased levels of debt.

The right has bitterly attacked "political correctness" in higher education but rarely mentions the economic side of the problem. The real threat to higher education comes from changes in the American economy. After all, the largest growth in higher education in recent years has, as Zachary Karabell points out, come from the "proliferation of preprofessional schools, from law to nursing, from hotel management to public health."[21] Whether or not they ever were, universities today are certainly not vine-covered ivory towers full of philosophers leading students in exercises of self-reflection (or, if you prefer, political correctness). Rather, they are places such as the University of Phoenix—an institution lacking buildings that offers its courses on-line to enhance students' business skills.[22] No wonder educational levels no longer correlate with political activity; no wonder

TABLE 3.2
AVERAGE CUMULATIVE STAFFORD DEBTS FOR UNDERGRADUATE STUDENTS, INCLUDING ACCRUED INTEREST ON UNSUBSIDIZED LOANS

Average Debt Level, 1999	% Change from 1998	% Change from 1995	Compounded Average % Change, 1995–1999
$10,173	3.5	19.0	4.4

Source: Patricia M. Scherschel, *Student Debt Levels Continue to Rise: Stafford Indebtedness: 1999 Updated*, USA Group, Inc., available at www.luminafoundation.org/Publications/pdfs/DebtBurden.pdf

educational institutions are no longer brimming with budding young idealists, the way many believed they were during the 1960s.[23] The idea that higher education helps enhance the critical skills of citizenship—questioning the way power works in society, and so forth—no longer seems prevalent. In the world of education, as in so many other places, the culture of self-seeking has replaced political engagement.

THE CIVIC CRISIS OF MEMBERSHIP-BASED POLITICAL ORGANIZATIONS: NOWHERE TO GO WHEN SCHOOL LETS OUT

Another significant change since the 1960s needs brief mention here. As already pointed out, the struggles of the 1960s left behind few permanent institutions. But something else changed as well— something traced out quite thoroughly by political scientists and sociologists such as Robert Putnam and Theda Skocpol. Political organizations on both the left and right have become increasingly "membership-based organizations"—the sort that require joiners simply to write a check every year and do very little else.[24] Political strategies that follow from this transformation have further marginalized ordinary citizens. As Margaret Weir and Marshall Ganz note, "From the 1970s on, advocacy organizations run by professional staff members at the state and national levels found that they could operate most effectively if they focused on single issues that could be addressed with specific insider strategies based on lobbying, litigation, and fund-raising."[25] In other words, participatory and citizen-based politics itself has ironically become professionalized, if not elite-based, over the past few years.

This has especially affected young people coming of political age during the 1980s and 1990s. First, it is easier today to lift one's nose at the mention of "special interest groups"—a feature of contemporary political discourse whereby every organization (be it the Association of Community Organizations for Reform Now [ACORN] or the Business Roundtable) appears sinister and corrupt. It also is more difficult for many young people to sense anything of a "public interest" operating within the Beltway. Most important of all, though, is the result of what I will call the "PIRG syndrome." As lobbying organizations become critical in politics and as public relations becomes more prevalent, young people typically get recruited into these public interest research organizations (PIRGs) solely for fund-raising pur-poses. That is, they are asked to knock on doors to canvass for money that will help support lobbying and advertising. Almost all of the young, progressive activists I spoke with for this project complained about burning out on a job as a canvasser for a PIRG or a group such as Citizen Action.[26] Thus, Putnam's civic crisis thesis has a special application to young people, especially those of a liberal and idealistic persuasion.

Chapter 4

THE WORLD OF
POLITICAL ARGUMENT:
CREATING A POLITICS OF GENERATION X

As young people have faced a changing political culture, pundits have latched onto their behavior as a harbinger of the end of politics as we know it. As Nina Eliasoph has argued, political apathy does not just happen. Rather, it is *willed* into existence—that is, the rejection of political awareness and activism is an *active* choice.[1] Many civic and political leaders as well as pundits have been encouraging public apathy and political disengagement. This anti-government stance goes hand in hand with a general shift of American politics to the right over the past few years.

Some political observers have been surprised by just how hard to the right American political discourse has shifted since the 1980s. Liberals have been shocked by the seriousness with which pundits and politicians take ideas such as the privatization of Social Security. It is hard to imagine such proposals taking off during the 1960s. Critical to the right's success have been the young pundits who dress up conservative ideas in "hip" political lingo. In addition, as grass-roots institutions have declined in importance in relation to American politics, media campaigns—many of them driven by money and charismatic personalities—have become that much more important. Though it is often hard to trace direct influence on policymaking, it is clear that pundits and the general media have had a much larger impact on American political discussion than they did thirty years ago.[2] Unfortunately, the center and even some progressives have helped diminish the relevance of government. After all, the Democratic Leadership Council (DLC)—which exerted a great deal of influence on the Clinton administration and still constitutes a major voice in the Democratic Party—has called for lessening governmental power. As Richard Kahlenberg and Ruy Teixeira write, "Current DLC documents call for privatizing Social Security, introducing Medicare vouchers, eliminating the national debt (greatly reducing funds available for public investment) and unleashing a new economy."[3] In shaping political discourse, pundits have helped encourage the already existing apathy of the younger generation.

CIVIC ORGANIZATIONS AND THE RISE OF A NEW NONCONSERVATIVE CONSERVATISM: GENERATION X'S ATTACK ON SOCIAL SECURITY

In 1992, Jonathan Cowan and Rob Nelson decided to create a membership-based organization that would address the political needs of Generation X. Their decision coincided with Ross Perot's run for the presidency, and Cowan and Nelson decided to attack Perot's enemy—the growing federal deficit. They named themselves "Lead or Leave" (LoL) and declared that politicians must either lower the deficit ("lead") or feel the pressure of young people (forcing politicians to "leave" if they did not comply with the plan). Despite the hopped-up and overblown promises and the organization's lack of any serious membership, the idea caught on, and Cowan and Nelson quickly became media darlings, their visages splashed across the cover of *Newsweek*. At photo-ops, they played up their stylish youthfulness, wearing baseball caps backwards and T-shirts. They even wrote a 1994 manifesto called *Revolution X*.

The book codified Generation X activism and political writing. It was simplistic, full of call-outs containing quotations or statistics taken out of context. It even had a note card with which readers could let President Clinton know their top political concerns. Cowan and Nelson began by rejecting the Gen X "slacker" stereotype, then pitted themselves against baby-boomer protesters: "No fire hoses, tear gas, police dogs, or riots. Let's face it: Most of us aren't looking for unnecessary confrontation."[4] Notice that they focused on the *styles* of protest movements, not the substantive points such movements were trying to make. The authors argued that the decade of the 1960s was too full of ideological partisanship and political conflict. Cowan and Nelson took note of a decline in political partisanship among their generation and then turned this into a fundamental principle of political faith. Generation X, in their words, was "postpartisan" and "pragmatic"—badges of honor, as far as the authors were concerned, and terms that would soon become fixtures in Gen X political coinage.

Of course, those who say they are not ideological or partisan are very often just that. Cowan and Nelson had a pretty clear political program. They took issue with the very basis of the American welfare state: "Our generation pays the highest relative taxes of any age group in America. Yet we get the fewest direct benefits."[5] While other analysts sifted through figures and set out thoughtful views of this complex issue, Cowan and Nelson focused more simply on fomenting distrust about the solvency of Social Security. Arguing that Social Security rang up a debt that would fall mainly on their generation, Cowan and Nelson equated it with the Vietnam War. They explained, "Our debt buildup has come to symbolize the slow and painful decay of America." As "the Great Depression and World War II became reference points for Americans in the 1930s and '40s" and as "civil rights and Vietnam for those raised in the 1960s," so Cowan and Nelson reasoned, "today's enormous national debt will define our opportunities and shape the choices open to our generation through the 1990s and beyond."[6] The analogy to Vietnam and World War II was debatable (if not preposterous), but this did not discourage them from making it. Cowan and Nelson threatened to rally youth, as they thought their predecessors had, around one noble cause and against older people.

Cowan and Nelson could not hold their organization together. Lead or Leave folded in 1995 amid bitter staff complaints about how the organization was run, lack of membership, and mismanagement of funds.[7] Though it failed in the short run, LoL actually left behind quite a large legacy. It had hit on a formula that successor Generation X political groups followed: attack Social Security in the name of "nonpartisan" youth and do so via a media strategy rather than building a grassroots movement. Cowan and Nelson created a new basis for conservative argumentation without sounding or appearing like older conservatives. As the 1990s proceeded, the tone of these complaints grew more bitter and drifted further to the right. During the mid-1990s, organization after organization formed under the banner of youth and with this exact purpose in mind. There was the Project for a New Generation, Generation X Coalition, the National Association of Twentysomethings, and X-PAC. Following the example of their predecessor, these organizations all went belly-up.

Only one group, Third Millennium (TM), outlasted the rest. Formed only a year after Lead or Leave, it released a manifesto, which the group imagined as an updated Port Huron Statement (though it lacked that document's political sophistication). TM founders declared themselves "postpartisan" and (like all Gen X'ers) were prone to use pop culture references. In ringing language they declared: "Like Wile E. Coyote, waiting for a 20-ton Acme anvil to fall on his head, our generation labors in the expanding shadow of a monstrous national debt."[8] TM had a single idea that it chanted like a mantra: privatize Social Security in the name of Generation X. As Richard Thau, executive director of TM, put it in a speech to the Cato Institute (not exactly known for its lack of partisanship), Social Security might seem like "social insurance" to the elderly, but for "my generation it is just another tax."

Third Millennium, unlike other short-lived Generation-X advocacy organizations, has no qualms about taking money from those with a self-interest in privatizing Social Security. TM has accepted contributions from the J. M. Kaplan Fund (a foundation that has supported numerous initiatives to privatize Social Security), the Coalition for Change (whose members include the Business Roundtable and the U.S. Chamber of Commerce), Merrill Lynch, and others. It might not be entirely fair to call TM a "front group," but it would not be too much of a stretch either; the money they have raised has given them access to the media and even to those with political power.

TM's leaders have testified before Congress to call for the privatization of Social Security and, more recently, Medicare. This sounds like touting the Republican Party platform. But TM argues (probably for tax purposes as much as anything else) that the organization "isn't liberal, moderate, or conservative, but post-partisan." Known best for its assertion that more young people believe in UFOs than in the solvency of Social Security (one of the most talked-about factoids in the history of polling), TM has gone on to "discover" that 53 percent of young Americans believe that the TV show *General Hospital* will outlast Medicare. With these polls, it has pioneered a new form of media-driven politics—speaking for young people through the seemingly

objective world of political polling. With typically questionable reasoning, TM argues that poll showings such as these are grounds
enough to gut social programs. TM leaders say that polling is neutral
and unbiased, though they contradict this through the political use to
which they put their polling. They have helped drive politics further
to the right in America—all the while speaking for supposedly post-
partisan Generation X.

THE POSTPARTISAN PUNDITRY:
OLD IDEAS IN NEW SHEEP'S CLOTHING

A new pundit—Meredith Bagby—has arisen out of TM. Bagby began
her career in the Ross Perot campaign and then moved into the ranks
of TM. At the same time, she started to write books and appear as a
commentator on CNN. She testified before Congress, arguing against
Medicare. Her most recent book, *We've Got Issues: The Get Real,
No. B.S., Guilt-Free Guide to What Really Matters*, is chock-full of
pictures of young people making ridiculous statements on American
politics (for instance, "Politics has become a kind of consumerism.
Mmmm . . . tasty," Eric Sequeira). Bagby explains that she and a com-
panion, Alden Levy, traveled down to Washington, D.C., to "represent
the young folks." Bagby claims she represented "all" young people.
"Even you. You didn't elect us to do the job? Tough luck. Someone
had to do it. . . . It was fun to sit in a big congressional room and
talk out of my bum."[9] This does not inspire confidence in her leadership capacities. Nor does much of anything else that Bagby writes.

Bagby's first book, *Rational Exuberance: The Influence of
Generation X on the New American Economy,* focused on
Generation X's capacity for entrepreneurship during the height of
the 1990s economic boom. She showcased her successful friends (with
attractive photographs), maintaining, "We [of Generation X] are
above all self-reliant and self-defining. We start our own companies at
a staggering rate" (of course, she did not take seriously the staggering
rate of business failure or the rise of slavish temp work among
Generation X). Bagby even suggested that entrepreneurship was more
important than political engagement. She declared, "We are accused
of being apathetic about using the voting booth. The truth is, we vote
every day, twenty four hours a day—with our dollars. . . . We make
and break industries by what we buy and refuse to buy."[10] Bagby

made clear that Generation X would find salvation in the private pursuits best facilitated by the corporate market. Political engagement should be ditched for the private world of consumerism.

The political implications of this "entrepreneurial" argument seem obvious. If young people are entrepreneurial and looking after themselves, what need have they for social programs? More important, Bagby argues that government is acting in the interests of the elderly and against those of Generation X. There is a peculiar displacement of class as a tool of sociopolitical analysis and an embrace of generation as a new tool. Using awkward, youthful slang, Bagby explains in her second book, *We've Got Issues*, "Our government is robbin' our collective 'hood by transferring huge quantities of money from young working Americans to the elderly. . . . And it ain't just in income where older people have a marked advantage. Old people have more stuff."[11] So instead of the problem being about rich and poor (this at a time when there are exorbitant amounts of economic inequality), the problem is now about young and old. The enemy is framed not as wealthy citizens abdicating their social responsibility but as the federal government taking money away from entrepreneurial Generation X'ers.

Bagby's arguments may sound flimsy, but they represent a new type of Generation X punditry that makes conservative arguments sound "hip" rather than old-fashioned (Bagby, too, calls herself postpartisan). In the late 1990s, the cable channel MSNBC did much to promote this new punditocracy. In analyzing the rise of young media stars such as Laura Ingraham and Omar Wasow, one journalist, Tad Friend, writing for the *New York Times Magazine* observed a "constellation of beliefs" among Generation X pundits. These included "suspicion of power; championing of individual rights; the conviction that free markets, rather than government regulation, create a model society." Friend chose to describe this constellation of beliefs as "neither left nor right. If anything, it is libertarian."[12] Of course, he fails to note that the right has become increasingly libertarian. This sort of political confusion—an inability to label what is clearly conservative conservative—has been sown by Generation X punditocracy.

A more impressive example of this new punditocracy is Michele Mitchell, a young writer who worked for the *New York Times* before she wrote *A New Kind of Party Animal: How the Young Are Tearing Up the American Political Landscape*. Mitchell's book looks more like a book than *Revolution X*, *Rational Exuberance*, or *We've Got*

American left should be about. During the 1980s, a number of them were active in the anti-interventionist and anti-nuclear movements. Indeed, students at Brown University during the 1980s put the issue of the nuclear arms buildup on the map by passing a suicide pill referendum—a policy that would have stockpiled cyanide tablets for possible use in case of nuclear war. By the late 1980s, most progressive activists had focused their attention on South African apartheid. Students at Ivy League colleges (especially Columbia and Cornell) led demonstrations in favor of divesting university funds from South Africa. These activists were clearly focused: they protested an unjust system while showing what an institution could do about it. For a while, the counterculture of the 1980s—punk rock and "alternative" music and cultural scenes—intersected with these causes, seemingly recreating the spirit of 1960s protest cultures.[27] Though these movements never got the attention that the 1960s New Left did (after all, this was the Reagan era), they made clear that student and youth activism on the left had not disappeared.

During the late 1980s and early 1990s, student activism shifted toward issues of multiculturalism and respect for diversity. Students demanded more representation of non-Western writers in the curriculum and argued against demeaning speech. Conservative intellectuals had a field day with this sort of thing; indeed, Dinesh D'Souza, author of *Illiberal Education*, created an entire career out of attacking "political correctness." As Paul Loeb documents, much of D'Souza's critique was unfounded, if not based on self-manufactured reports.[28] Needless to say, though, this movement's focus on language and personal behavior did seem limited in ambition, if not entirely apolitical. Critics from the left—Russell Jacoby and Todd Gitlin—criticized the constraints of "identity politics" and multiculturalism. As Gitlin quipped, the left seemed to march on English departments at a time when the right was seizing Washington.[29]

Around the same time, the labor movement was getting back on its feet. John Sweeney, the AFL-CIO president, decided to make the goal of "organizing the unorganized" paramount. Others within the AFL-CIO leadership saw potential in student and youth activism, if only it could be harnessed for labor organizing. In 1996, the AFL-CIO launched Union Summer, a program that placed young people on organizing drives for a summer. As the head of Union Summer, Andy Levin, explained, "Put simply, we want to inject a massive dose of class consciousness into youth politics."[30] There were numerous drawbacks to the program: too many people entered some sites, and often there was not enough follow-up. With this said, however, there were numerous successes. In the first year, there were Union Summer projects in twenty cities. More than one thousand participants were exposed to the ins and outs of union organizing—running campaigns, organizing communities. Young people, many of them from the ranks of the middle class, were exposed to the plights of the working poor. Some of the students stayed on and joined the labor movement full time. Some were exposed to wider debates about progressivism in America, and it was clear that young people—not *all* young people, of course—could be drawn back into a responsible left.[31]

New involvement in the labor movement took a special form on America's campuses. Students started demanding that the clothing sold in campus stores (often containing the emblem of a college sports team) no longer be made with sweatshop labor. As Liza Featherstone, a journalist sympathetic to the movement, pointed out, "Protests forced more than fifty universities and colleges to capitulate to students' demands and join the Worker Rights Consortium (WRC), an organization independent of apparel-industry influence and founded in April by students as an alternative to the Fair Labor Association (FLA), an industry backed monitoring group."[32] This cause has galvanized a great deal of student energy. I interviewed one activist at the University of Oregon who had led the struggle for the recognition of the WRC there. He had come out of previous struggles around multicultural sensitivity. The transition from multicultural to economic activism seemed natural to him; after all, most sweatshop laborers are minorities, at least as perceived from an American perspective.[33]

At its best, this movement has also taken note of the labor struggles within academia, as this generation faces what can only be called an "academic labor crisis." Many recent Ph.D.s are not finding full-time teaching positions precisely because of universities' increased reliance on underpaid adjunct (that is, part-time) professors and graduate students in place of tenure-track professors, mirroring the overall trend toward "temp" employment. More than half of university teaching is now off the tenure track. Recently, graduate students at New York University (NYU) and other institutions have fought back and demanded recognition as "workers" under the National Labor Relations Act. This movement recognizes that the university is increasingly acting like a cutthroat corporation, not just outside its own walls but internally. Within the academic labor movement, leaders have articulated a stinging critique of the temping of America. The fact that graduate students and undergraduate sympathizers have rallied around this cause goes to show that economic justice is inspiring growing numbers of young activists.[34]

The student anti-sweatshop struggle and the academic labor movement are both clearly focused, and underlying them is a growing concern about the power of corporations in the process of globalization. This was most evocatively witnessed in the unexpectedly popular protests against the World Trade Organization (WTO) in Seattle. Anti-corporatism seems an understandable cause. After all, this generation has witnessed an enormous amount of corporate centralization, especially within what Mark Krispin Miller calls the "entertainment state." Young people have been exposed to thousands of advertisements to the point of jadedness and irony and have been target marketed like no other generation before.[35] Though many young people are apathetic about the moral and political consequences of consumerism and globalization (and have become enamored with business in the process), it is not surprising that those who are disgruntled target corporations. United Students Against Sweatshops declares that it is building a "grassroots student movement that challenges corporate power."[36] The Movement for Democracy, another student organization, describes itself as blatantly anti-corporate.[37]

In the struggles against sweatshop labor, what might have remained a diffuse attitude of anti-corporatism has become focused and reformist. Students offer a set of standards that they think should apply to products sold in the university's stores. But at other times, the rhetoric of organizations such as the Movement for Democracy can become overblown. Sounding as if they are cribbing from Frankfurt School Cliff Notes, the authors of a Movement for Democracy statement write: "The universities, colleges, and schools of the 90s have themselves become fully corporate, authoritarian, and anti-democratic. Our very minds are colonized by the corporate lie. Unless our schools, and society at large, are removed from corporate control, how can any individual person live free? The task ahead of us, those who would find justice in our time, is to end the rule of the corporation."[38] It is not clear if these students are embracing a socialist alternative (whatever form that would take), but it is clear that their grandiose claims do not square too well with the more reformist tendencies of the anti-sweatshop movement. Liza Featherstone recognized a tension within United

Students Against Sweatshops between revolutionary anarchists and reformists.[39]

Many supporters are most enthusiastic about the internationalist tendency of the movement—the fact that young American college students are concerned with sweatshop workers in Malaysia, for instance. But while internationalist rhetoric may be appealing, it is logistically problematic. In the movements of the 1960s, citizens tried to get their government to change existing policy (that is, to stop a war or abolish segregation). The civil rights movement succeeded because it was able to appeal to shared American values such as democracy and equality. Many of today's activists focus their sights on increasingly global bodies—organizations such as the WTO and IMF—whose primary constituents may not share this set of values. Certainly, some of the leaders of the G-8 have conceded the relevance of universal cries of debt relief, but there is still quite a way to go on this front. There is a great deal of talk about building a global civil society in order to counteract the power of corporations, but there is very little clear thinking on how to build the sort of solidarity necessary to do this.

There is also the threat that the movement will become enamored of boycotts that can turn distinctly apolitical. Alongside global awareness has risen the practice of concerned consumerism, probably most popularly represented in the Body Shop. There is something good about this: private institutions certainly have a role to play in creating a more just society. But we risk losing sight of the need for public figures who are accountable to citizens to monitor social justice. This becomes especially critical when one considers that a citizen's relation to existing public institutions at the global level is extremely vague. The new global activists need to think hard about what set of representative political institutions they can appeal to in order to make an impact.[40]

Chapter 5

WHAT CAN BE DONE?

One thing is clear: Generation X's beliefs and behavior are diffuse. This generation holds a broad range of political beliefs—everything from conservatism (more often libertarian in nature than cultural) to anti-corporate leftist sentiments for social justice. It is therefore unfair to draw sweeping generalizations about young people and politics today. Nonetheless, there are some concerns that cut across all political beliefs: Young people as a whole are turning away from traditional political participation, partly because of an assault on traditional politics that has come mostly from the right. This is most clearly reflected in a lack of partisanship and knowledge about political issues. Even those we would normally expect to be politically engaged are not. For instance, both young people who perform service and young, progressive activists are prone to inactivity in the realm of more conventional politics. Activists express hostility and suspicion about electoral politics, despite the fact that their work assumes the need for responsiveness on the part of elected officials. (One young environmentalist working on the Alaska Wildlife Refuge issue told me he was not concerned with the outcome of the presidential election of 2000.) The few activists I spoke with who *did* care about electoral politics expressed exasperation about the lack of political commitment on the part of other activists.

The process of attracting young people to public life is one means to revive progressive politics. This is not because youthful idealism always tends leftward (as young people made clear when they voted for Reagan during the 1980s) but because the present-day distrust of government by youth makes progressive politics more difficult. To correct for the injustices of the day—lack of health care, unfair labor practices, environmental degradation—we need a stronger government and a sense that the government works for the public good. We should develop a twofold strategy that will reconnect young people to public life and democratic action while pointing out that there is a progressive alternative to the right's dominant political vision.

Much of what I discuss here draws from my own activity as research and associate director of the Walt Whitman Center for the Culture and Politics of Democracy at Rutgers University from 1995 to 2001. In my work at the center, I was constantly approached by progressive organizations that were trying to involve young people in public and civic life. As a result, I have developed a number of ideas—discussed here in no particular order and with varying amounts of attention. These ideas are not, of course, the last word on the subject; rather, I hope they will provoke further research and experimentation.

TRADITIONAL CIVIC EDUCATION—AND BEYOND

One of the easiest places to introduce young people to politics is in school. During the nineteenth century, civic education was pursued through the study of history—that is, the memorization of certain historical facts taken as essential for citizenship in a republic (often facts about previous republics and the founding of America). By the early twentieth century, the social sciences began to displace history in academia. This change filtered down to high schools. From the 1930s to 1950s, civic education became equated with "social studies," an amalgamation of different social science disciplines. The idea that social studies provided the best source for civic education came under criticism in the 1980s, however, and has never truly recovered.

In 1988, the Center for Civic Education and the Council for the Advancement of Citizenship released a report that assessed civic education at the high school level. The report was gloomy: "The question of what citizenship means was seldom addressed. Little was said about the aims of citizenship education. Descriptions of civic education as a subject tend toward conceptual fuzziness and diffusion. In only a few instances could a specific rationale for civic education be found."[1] The Center for Civic Education then went on to put forth a proposed set of national standards, published in *Civitas: A*

Framework for Civic Education. In 1992, the federal government followed suit by creating its own set of standards through the passage of Goals 2000, otherwise known as the Educate America Act. It is debatable how effective either of these two initiatives has been.

There are numerous reasons why civic education has fallen into disarray and why some are pessimistic about any renewed call to standards to guide its renewal. First, standards in education—though much more popular today than in the 1960s—have always made many educators suspicious. Teachers complain about "teaching to the test" and turning learning into rote memorization. Besides, piling up a new set of demands on already overcommitted teachers creates understandable tension. Many critics also worry that, in a pluralistic society, common civic standards are difficult to define. (For instance, should we teach patriotism or civil disobedience?) Although others believe there are core civic standards, this debate makes clear how difficult it is to achieve consensus. In addition, there are so many different ways of approaching civic education—public service, experiential education, internships, formal lessons about how government works, and more—that it is difficult to get agreement among educators on the best method. Because of these conflicts, grounds for optimism about a renewal of civic education at the K–12 levels seem faint at best.

Opinions differ on whether the traditional civic education of yesteryear helped raise levels of political connectedness.[2] Perhaps the best way to move beyond this debate is to combine traditional civic education—some basic factual knowledge about the way American government works—and experiential education—allowing young people the opportunity to learn from community engagement. On this front, there seems to be some reason for hope. For instance, there is Kids Voting, a program that encourages young people to get their parents to take them voting. Teachers work with students on the project and give them general civic lessons along the way. This program has effectively involved young people in political education through family and community life and then merged this with more formal knowledge conveyed by teachers.[3] Another organization, Youth Vote 2000, has raised levels of voting by doing something as simple as making one-on-one phone calls to young people eligible to vote—prompting them to think about issues they care about and how those issues related to political choices in the voting booth. This was "estimated to have caused a 13.3 percentage point jump in the probability of voting."[4] Clearly, simple political discussion (with peers or parents) can enhance young people's interest in politics.

Unfortunately, some civic education programs outside of the world of schools take on the worst features of youth culture. Rock the Vote probably best exemplifies this. This organization, founded in 1990, received most of its funding from Warner Brothers and Capitol Records (as well as other corporations with an interest in the youth market). Its cofounder explained in 1992 that the group intended "to raise the political consciousness of kids and to make voting hip."[5] The first problem occurred when its major spokespeople—figures such as Madonna, who went on television draped in a flag to tell young people to vote—were discovered not to be registered to vote themselves.[6] This did little to overcome political cynicism. Even worse, however, is the slippery line between the noble act of increasing the vote and the corporate sponsors' self-interest. A spokesperson for Coors, another funder of Rock the Vote, explained, "I'm not going to sit here and try to tell you this is about voting. We're talking about selling beer and decided we could kill two birds with one stone."[7] In this day and age, it is probably safe to assume that young people receive the message to buy things even when it is latched onto the message to vote; it is easy to imagine them failing to hear Madonna begging them to vote and rather thinking about buying her next CD. Programs that move outside the walls of the traditional school need to be aware of the pernicious qualities of our consumer culture (something that Clinton's presidential summit ignored). It is doubtful how successful Rock the Vote has been in increasing young people's connection to politics.[8]

MOVING BEYOND THE DISCONNECT:
RECONNECTING VOLUNTARY SERVICE AND POLITICAL EDUCATION

With this danger in mind, it still seems best to approach young people about politics both within and outside the formal setting of schools. And today one of the best places to do this is whenever they perform public service. If participants in service programs can see the connections between their service and the wider world of public policy, then these programs will cultivate more engaged and thoughtful citizens. This requires more attention to the educational aspects of service.

There is some reason for hope here. Many colleges and universities have instituted what are called "service-learning programs." Students enrolled in these programs perform service but also discuss what they are doing in the classroom. They might, for instance, take a class on housing policy while working at a homeless shelter. Students then connect what they are doing at their service site with the bigger policy changes that shape or should shape their efforts. In studying these programs, researchers have found that students walk away with a deeper understanding of social issues and their political implications. Researchers (including myself) have found that programs with poor-quality classroom components increased students' levels of cynicism or detachment. But when the connections are made well, students do in fact increase their civic and political knowledge.[9]

This should provide us with hope for injecting an educational component into the many public service programs sprouting up in America today. During the past six years, I have worked with public service organizations to do precisely this. Margo Shea and I discovered that by simply discussing public service and its consequences, participants almost always made connections to wider political issues.[10] For instance, in 1997 I worked with participants in Public Allies in Wilmington, Delaware. This group was at first hostile to political discussion. One woman told me in our first meeting that she thought the term politics came from the combination of two different words: polis, which meant public (a correct definition) and ticks, those who leech off the public good. (Whether that part of her definition is correct depends, of course, on your outlook.) Most of the participants, almost all of whom had college educations, told me that they never voted—which should not surprise us. But they were eager, as were other members of their generation, to perform public service.

I met with this group for a year, and by the end of it, many of their attitudes had changed. First, they started making connections between their service and local and national politics. One woman who worked in a transitional housing program discovered that there had been a whole host of reforms, both local and national, that made it more difficult for her to do her work. She decided to continue her service work while also scanning the horizon for political changes. At the conclusion of her one-year assignment, she believed that at some point she would need to go into advocacy work in order to protect the programs she had helped out with during her service. The woman who coined the term *poli-ticks* went through a similar experience. It would be presumptuous of me to claim that discussing issues during the course of the year was the sole reason for these young people's changed attitudes. But I am quite certain that without this opportunity many more of the participants would have remained locked in the cynical stage in which they began.

There are certainly some service programs that do a better job than others at making connections between service and political change. As two researchers, Joel Westheimer and Joseph Kahne, have pointed out, different organizations have very different ways of conceptualizing the goal of service. Drawing on a number of years of study for the Surdna Foundation, these researchers differentiate between those who conceive of service producing a "personally responsible citizen," a "participatory citizen," or a "justice-oriented citizen." The first "works and pays taxes, obeys laws, and helps those in need during crises such as snowstorms and floods." The second "actively participates in the civic affairs and the social life of the community at local, state, and national levels." The third "critically assesses social, political, and economic structures and explores collective strategies for change that challenge injustice and, when possible, addresses root causes of problems." As Westheimer and Kahne see it, these very different conceptions of citizenship help shape the outcomes of service programs.[11]

Westheimer and Kahne have found, perhaps not surprisingly, that programs with a justice-oriented model connect service participation to wider political engagement more effectively than others. By asking participants to think about how their service relates to wider issues (done through discussion, often moderated by a teacher), these programs show both the power and limitations of service. Young people understand what their service can and cannot accomplish. These programs also make sure that young people—even if they do not necessarily act on this knowledge immediately—at least think about what could be done at the larger level of policy to tackle problems they have encountered in service.

Even with all of this in mind, those voluntary programs that emphasize the connection between service and politics still draw from the "self-selecting" population. That is, they entice young people already committed to the ideals of service. Young middle-class participants remain "do-gooders" and view those being served as "clients" at best. Those who are disaffected and perhaps most in need of such experiences do not join.

Fortunately, there are now programs in place that attempt to overcome this problem. From 1998 to 2000, I observed a program in Philadelphia that deserves attention precisely because it challenges growing inequalities and civic disaffection while also drawing out the political implications of service. The Center for Greater Philadelphia, housed at the University of Pennsylvania, has recently created what it calls a High School Partnership Project. This program brings students from inner-city schools (typically underfunded and thus poor) and students from suburban schools (typically quite well off) together to work on public service projects, such as cleaning up a public park or helping out a nonprofit organization. The program teaches important lessons to young people about the relation between socioeconomic inequality and the decline of American civic life. It also cuts against the tendency of middle-class do-gooders to see themselves as superior to those being served.

Young people in this program were forced to confront the disparities in their lives. During one group meeting, for instance, private school students assumed that everyone owned a computer and that the group could therefore create a website as a part of their project. The public school students admitted to not owning computers, which created an embarrassing situation that once again made it difficult for these students to work together but also forced them to think about inequality in a constructive manner.

In another case, students started to discuss what sort of projects they wanted to work on. Students from a wealthy suburban school wanted to focus on youth violence. Immediately, students from the inner-city school hedged on the project, arguing that youth violence is often puffed up by the mass media. They started giving examples of how news media trucks would zoom into their neighborhood any time an act of violence took place. The inner-city students were tired of focusing on violence, not because they denied its existence but because of how it fit into a stereotype of their neighborhoods and fellow citizens. In trying to come together in their public work, the students were left looking at a widening chasm—and at all of the ramifications of this divide.

In one group, students were exposed to the problems of pollution in their communities. These students started to recognize a link between their service and questions concerning public policy and saw the role that local citizen action could (and could not) play in problem solving. Of course, the service itself did not promise to be anything more than a temporary intervention; it was in discussion that students identified potential, long-term citizen action solutions and associated their work with wider civic possibilities. In another group meeting, the Partnership staff asked a group to discuss a social issue discovered in the process of service. The group, which worked on a variety of projects throughout Philadelphia, focused on "people moving out of the city into the suburbs." An exceptionally bright student from a suburban school argued that during the 1930s and 1940s "homes were segregated by street, but not by neighborhood." This initiated a debate about earlier segregation that became a general conversation about redlining and suburban sprawl. The discussion was quite sophisticated, with allusions to public policy and urban patterns and, eventually, taxation. Yet it never became too abstract because a teacher asked the students to think about their parents' attitudes toward taxation. All in all, it was a productive conversation on some major questions about socioeconomic inequality, and it showed that students from different backgrounds could work together to connect service to public policy.[12]

Nonetheless, this program in Philadelphia and the ones that Westheimer and Kahne discussed are exceptions. Most service programs are pressed for time and barely succeed in getting their participants to perform the necessary number of service hours, let alone talk and think about their work. Making wider connections seems like too much work (as many of those I worked with over the past few years have complained). Programs like AmeriCorps try to cut young people off from politics entirely. Those that try to tie service to wider political issues may be accused of being *too political*—of being indoctrination camps into left-wing causes. This is certainly a problem, but the alternative—allowing young people to see service as isolated from politics—seems too steep a price to pay. Service program leaders need to think critically and thoughtfully about how they can relate experiences in public service to politics. The fact that it can and has been done should provide some hope.

CREATING SPACES IN WHICH TO NURTURE THE NEXT GENERATION OF ACTIVISTS AND INTELLECTUALS

The idea of "mentoring" has caught on among a generation that performs increasing amounts of voluntary service. For good reason, too, since a flesh-and-blood example is often most inspiring for young people. The case can easily be extended to the world of politics. As one researcher points out, internships with elected officials often raise levels of knowledge, sophistication, and a sense of connectedness to the political system.[13] Under the auspices of the New Jersey Civic Education Network, politicians have met with high school students to talk about their work and its relation to the public good. Though there has been little analysis of the effectiveness of this initiative, the amount of interest on the part of local politicians suggests that it brings at least some long-term rewards. As one politician explained it to me, mentoring took time, but he focused on the long-term impact of having a constituency that was more educated. He saw little immediate payoff but instead stressed his responsibility for training future leaders.[14]

Echoing this sentiment, numerous colleges have created "leadership schools" in recent years. These are typically summer institutes where high school students gather together to do "mock legislatures" and other exercises in political education.[15] Politicians often lecture at these leadership schools. Though these programs are quite effective at engaging young people, they are limited to the elite. A scholarship program would make these sorts of experiences available to poorer young people—those who, after all, are most likely to feel disaffected from American politics.

The mentoring that leadership schools have set up with elected officials needs to be extended to the world of grassroots and community organizing since this world seems to attract those disaffected from traditional political paths. Although, many activists I interviewed had *bad* experiences with progressive organizations (as in the canvassing positions mentioned previously), others stressed the importance of mentors in their lives. Wendy Ray, who presently works as a program director for U.S. Action (the successor to Citizen Action), discussed the importance to her of Heather Booth, an activist who came out of struggles of the 1960s and remains committed to community organizing and the Democratic Party today (and who runs a community organizing training school, the Midwest Academy). Ray explained how Booth worked with her on campaigns and taught her the ins and outs of organizing. Ray also was impressed when Booth invited numerous young people to come to her house for dinner and political discussions. By personal example, Booth made the possibility of engaged citizenship seem more "real," as Ray put it, and helped her make the transition to full-time activism. (Another young activist

I spoke with echoed this sentiment about mentors more generally.) All of the activists that I interviewed argued that progressive organizations should do a better job at welcoming and mentoring young people rather than simply plugging them into entry-level positions. (They did admit, though, that this would require a great deal of time.)[16]

What young activists (and yes, there *are* young activists out there) need is an institution or place where they can learn what works best from veteran organizers. They also need a space where they can link their activism to bigger ideas about political change—the way public service participants need to link their work to a wider discussion about politics. To counteract a tendency toward "issues" politics among activists or, quite simply, toward bad ideas, we need places where connections are being made, where a sense of the wider picture can be developed.

Plenty of historians and political observers have pointed out how the right won the war of ideas during the 1970s and 1980s by creating a slew of think tanks where ideas could be both developed and distributed. The Heritage Foundation, the American Enterprise Institute, the Olin Foundation, and other organizations have had an enormous impact on the way Americans discuss political issues and policies (as I have shown, they also have shaped the way we think about Generation X). Numerous critics have pointed out that there is no equivalent to these institutions on the left (the closest places that exist, the New America Foundation and Demos, do not identify themselves as progressive and are too new to have their impact assessed).[17] There would seem to be an easy solution to the problem: more funding for progressive think tanks, which can employ and nurture younger thinkers and writers and bring these thinkers together with activists. But this is easier said than done. First, there is a lack of financial support available for organizations on the left. Private foundations have shown an uneasiness about funding initiatives that lack a clear-cut impact. And the world of ideas and debate is a murky one. When I once tried to raise funds for a fledgling magazine, one sympathetic foundation officer told me that my cause was hopeless. Magazines, think tanks, and any institutions engaged in the production of ideas were perceived as "black holes" by funders—meaning they had little in the way of identifiable outcomes, unlike programs that fed homeless people or mentored young people.

But the problem goes deeper than lack of funding. The world of writing has changed for the worse over the past few years. In his provocative book, *The Last Intellectuals,* Russell Jacoby argued that academia—with its emphasis on intellectual specialization and obtuse jargon—had swallowed up what he called "public intellectuals." The public intellectuals of yesteryear—those like Richard Hofstadter, Irving Howe, and Daniel Bell—often held academic positions but in a day and age when such positions allowed time for writing outside of academia. Today, young academics are too busy writing an enormous number of articles for increasingly specialized journals that are read —if at all—by a small set of academics schooled in the requisite terminology. At the same time, they are expected to teach an increasing number of classes (teaching loads nowadays go up to five courses per semester), often at numerous different institutions (the "expressway adjunct professor" phenomenon).[18]

Unfortunately, the world of popular writing, with its sensationalism and its corporate bottom line, does not seem any more conducive to writing about important political questions. Indeed, it seems increasingly difficult for young writers to imagine writing in a manner that is neither academic—that is, narrow and inaccessible—nor in the worst sense popular—that is, superficial and self-revealing. At a gathering of young writers being recruited by *Dissent* magazine, the journal's editors talked up their tradition of "literary journalism," a way of writing intended both to analyze and to be read by more than academic peers. The young people in the room seemed bewildered but also intrigued. The fact that *Dissent*'s American readership has declined (as has the readership for other small magazines) simply highlights my general point.

How then can a young writer take up difficult and important topics without tending toward academic specialization or journalism's simplicity? It seems increasingly difficult in this day and age. That is why any future center will need to think of ways to entice young writers away from academia while also promising to find popular outlets for their writing (something that the New America Foundation, whose politics is all over the place, has been trying to do). Whether or not there will remain a reading public for serious political writing remains to be seen, especially as the media continues to merge politics and entertainment. Undoubtedly, a great deal of the publishing from any future think tank will have to take place on the Internet in order to attract a new set of younger readers. With an increased emphasis on pragmatism in youth politics—the embrace of hands-on service over politics—it will certainly become difficult to explain the importance of ideas and vision. That is why a center or think tank that could bring activists together with writers and intellectuals could satisfy those young people who are searching for something more than just politicians intent on winning office.

REFORMING THE POLITICAL SYSTEM

Report after report shows that young people view politics as corrupt. On this issue, Generation X is neither wrong nor out of sync with the rest of America. With the increased attention to scandals—some of them personal but many of them financial—it is not surprising that young people reject politics. No amount of moral hand-wringing will bring Generation X back. We need to take this generation's disaffection seriously. After all, American politics *is* corrupt. So many citizens reacted favorably to John McCain's run for president—and this sympathy was felt across partisan loyalties—because he honestly addressed the issue of political corruption and argued for doing something about it. Though there is no hard evidence for this, I believe that also is why many young people were attracted to McCain.

To bring young people back, we need to follow John McCain's clarion call: Get money out of politics. (It goes without saying that the recent Enron scandal only highlights this need.) We seem to be forever at the cusp of winning some sort of reform. Campaign finance reform will not solve all problems in American politics (lobbyists and politicians are already looking for loopholes in proposed legislation). But without it we cannot expect young people to reengage in politics.

Of course, we should not stop with campaign finance reform. We need to think about other reforms, like expanding voter registration and education programs, experimenting with proportional representation, and opening up political debates to third-party candidates. Indeed, we need to widen the debate about the possibilities of political reform. None of the reforms mentioned here will necessarily attract massive numbers of young people back to the voting booths. But they would certainly make it more difficult for young people to justify their disengagement. This just might be one of the most important reasons to engage in reform today. Young people's disaffection with politics today should serve as a spur toward a revival of progressive reform aimed at getting money out of politics and making government more responsive to ordinary citizens.

It probably sounds odd to bring up political parties in the context of young people and political participation. After all, this is the most nonpartisan generation in American history. As Ted Halstead recently pointed out, "Surveys suggest that no more than a third of young adults identify with either political party, and only a quarter vote a straight party ticket."[19] But the response to this phenomenon on the part of pundits seems murky and shortsighted at best. Recall Ralph Nader's presidential campaign on the Green Party ticket (which attracted numerous young people). His run was premised on a post-partisan argument about a lack of difference between the Democrats and Republicans (he used the term Republicrats). This, quite simply, ignores reality on a number of vital issues: Social Security, education, policies toward labor unions, the environment, regulation of corporations, and taxation. Many of these issues matter to young people—not only at the level of ideals (environmentalism shows up again and again as a key "youth" issue) but also at the level of self-interest (education and taxation). As political parties have reduced themselves to fund-raising engines, they have neglected the role of political education outside the context of winning elections. For this reason, many young people see political parties as corrupt institutions serving "special interests" rather than as organizations that embody a political vision in the interest of ordinary citizens.

Here I think it is important to recall a lesson from history. During the late 1960s, many activists within the Democratic Party grew disgruntled with Lyndon Baines Johnson and his continued pursuit of the Vietnam War. Allard Lowenstein, who had previously been president of the National Student Association, led the "Dump Johnson" movement. One activist and intellectual involved with this initiative, Arnold Kaufman, argued that a focus solely on winning elections damaged the party's long-term interests. The Vietnam War and the Democrats' moral culpability in it had heightened the need for a politics of principle, as Kaufman saw it. For him, this required widening the purpose of the political party. As he outlined it in a set of notes on the New Democratic Coalition (an organization within the party that set itself against Hubert Humphrey), Kaufman set out (if cryptically) the following principles: "Radical reconstruction without abandoning or repudiating established political processes. Issues not candidates. Political education—principal task." Instead of being obsessed with electoral victories, the party should focus on the "education of publics" and "issue development." Kaufman argued, "Power, not trust, must be our principal aim within the New Democratic Coalition. . . . But power without trust corrupts our cause and debases our people."[20] Kaufman was not *against* winning elections, of course; he simply believed that the party needed to be about more than this if it wanted to be an effective political institution.

In many ways, I believe we need to renew Kaufman's idea about the Democratic Party and the general principles that stand behind it. Political parties need to participate in a debate about wider political vision (something that was started recently within Democratic ranks by the Democratic Leadership Council). They need to define their principles more starkly so that young people can understand why policy issues like Social Security and campaign finance reform matter. The Democratic Party, in particular, needs to make its public values more clear. For instance, during his presidential campaign, Al Gore failed when he talked about Social Security solely as something that affected old people. Had he focused on the program's commitment to cross-generational indebtedness, he might have attracted more young people to the party. At the least, it would have allowed more young people to start making sense of critical debates about American politics and differing political philosophies.

New roles must be created for young people within political parties. Only in this way can we break the circle of disengagement whereby political parties fail to reach out or spend the time educating young people because youth, as it is understood so well, do not vote. In order to attract young people, the political party needs to begin shifting its attention toward more grassroots educational efforts such as visits to college campuses. Grassroots and education-based campaigns often succeed even in our media-saturated political culture (in terms of both getting candidates elected and defeating highly funded initiatives in states like California). They also might be able to show young people that not all politics has to be about "spin."

Chapter 6

CONCLUSION

Youth apathy about politics is a multifaceted problem that requires a diverse set of responses. The problem cannot be divorced from the wider context of American politics—from the corruption of politics by money and the rightward drift of political debate since the 1980s. Many of the reforms I suggest here are incomplete, and none of them will ensure a massive upswing in youth participation or a rebirth of progressive politics. Nonetheless, they do suggest that youth disengagement matters and demands our attention. I do not believe we should shrug our shoulders at declines in civic and political participation among Generation X. This generation really does seem disaffected from the idea that traditional politics and political education matter. What we need to do is *reinject politics* into the way young people think about their worlds—in the realms of service and activism especially. While never belittling the importance of public service, we need to show that doing good on the individual level cannot address broader problems of inequality. Only then can we reengage young people in politics and, in the process, try to revive progressivism in America. The future (or lack thereof) of progressive politics and the attitudes of young people are inherently intertwined.

We must, however, reject those who argue that young people's behavior somehow signifies the need for massive transformations in the way we think about politics. The most recent exemplar of this line of reasoning is Andrei Cherny, author of *The Next Deal: The Future of Public Life in the Information Age*. A young member of the

Democratic Leadership Council (he helps edit *Blueprint* magazine),
Cherny has written a book that is overblown in a way that charac-
terizes a broader tendency in American intellectual life. He identifies
a new generation affected by something called a "Choice Revolution,"
symbolized by the Internet (an invention that has never failed to create exaggerated prognostications). Cherny argues that the Internet
places a new generation "in control." He provides the sterling example of Barbie.com, where young people "can design their own doll to
fit the specifications they choose." Young people, he explains, are
impatient, and their governmental institutions should reflect this principle: "A generation that impatiently raps its fingers on the table
when it takes more than a few seconds to download a web page from
China, which expects packages sent from the other end of the conti-
nent to arrive by 10:00 A.M. the next morning, which finds it difficult
to watch TV without a remote control in hand, which demands a
piping hot pizza delivered to their front door in half an hour, has
elected to bypass government through the immediacy of individual
action." Once again, a young pundit (this time seemingly on the left
end of the spectrum) suggests that government is just not "hip"
enough for the Gen X set. Cherny believes that this new generation
should simply vote for policies directly over the Internet. Nothing
should stand in the way of "individual empowerment." Like Meredith
Bagby and others, Cherny tries to draws far too many political lessons
from the peculiar behaviors of a new generation. This is not the sort
of political philosophy that we need today.[1]

I do not believe that we need to throw aside "old" institutions
like government, nor do I think we should encourage young people to
think that buying things on the Internet is anything like participating
in a democratic society with a vibrant public life. Instead, we need to
show how older institutions (including government) and principles
(including liberalism) still have something to teach us today. Though
Cherny seems to embrace impatience with the slowness of political
change, I would suggest that solutions to the inequalities of the new
economy will actually take time and require long-term initiatives car-
ried through in our governmental institutions and local community
life. We need a progressive vision that shows how both elements matter; local community service can help do good by providing services
to the disadvantaged and by educating young people about civic participation, while national governmental policies still have a role to
play in improving our collective lives.

Reconnecting public service with politics is a good start, for in doing so, we can get young people to see how everyday activities like working in a soup kitchen relate to the wider world of public policy and the traditional world of electoral politics. They can see firsthand how the smallness and delicacy of their individual acts of service are not enough to resolve the bigger problems they are confronting. In order to bring young people back to politics, we especially need to reform our political institutions—ridding them of the corrupt influence of money and instituting a more deliberative form of politics, one that includes reinvigorated parties. We need to think of ways in which the idea of politics and the public sector can be made meaningful to young people today. None of the reforms suggested here will necessarily result in young people suddenly rushing to the polls and turning into engaged citizens determined to improve our public life. But we will not know until we try.

NOTES

CHAPTER 1

1. Elizabeth Hubbard, "Defy Convention: Court Young Voters," *Philadelphia Inquirer* (November 1, 1998), available at the Pew Charitable Trusts Website, www.pewtrusts.com.

2. See Ted Halstead, "A Politics for Generation X," *The Atlantic Monthly*, August 1, 1999, pp. 33–42, and Stephen Craig and Stephen Bennett, *After the Boom: The Politics of Generation X* (Lanham, Md.: Rowman and Littlefield, 1997).

3. See www.youthvote2000.org for recent figures.

4. Sheilah Mann, "What the Survey of American College Freshmen Tells Us about Their Interest in Politics and Political Science," *PS: Political Science and Politics*, June 1999, p. 263.

5. Robert Putnam, *Bowling Alone: The Collapse and Revival of American Community* (New York: Simon and Schuster, 2000), p. 261.

6. Lisa Rathke, "U.S. Senator John McCain Addresses Vermont State Republican Convention," Associated Press, May 20, 2000.

7. Hart Research Associates, "America Unplugged: Citizens and Their Government." Poll conducted for the Council for Excellence in Government, available at www.excelgov.org.

8. Ruy Teixeira, *The Disappearing American Voter* (Washington, D.C.: Brookings Institution, 1992), p. 31.

9. Putnam, *Bowling Alone*, p. 247.

10. Steven Rosenstone and John Hansen, *Mobilization, Participation, and Democracy in America* (New York: MacMillan, 1993), pp. 136–37.

11. Craig and Bennett, *After the Boom*, p. 104.

12. Liza Featherstone, "The Student Movement Comes of Age," *The Nation*, October 16, 2000, pp. 23–26.

13. Putnam, *Bowling Alone*, p. 133.

14. See the National Association of Secretaries of State, "New Millenium Project—Phase I: A Nationwide Study of 15–24 Year Old Youth," available at NASS Website, www.nass.org, 1999, pp. 17–18.

CHAPTER 2

1. David Greenberg, "In the Shadow of the Sixties," in *Next: Young American Writers on the New Generation,* ed. Eric Liu (New York: Norton, 1994).

2. Alan Brinkley, "The Therapeutic Radicalism of the New Left," in his *Liberalism and Its Discontents* (Cambridge: Harvard University Press, 1998), p. 232.

3. Moses quoted in Taylor Branch, *Pillar of Fire: America in the King Years, 1963–65* (New York: Simon and Schuster, 1998), p. 474. Branch's quote is found on p. 475.

4. On Lowenstein, see William Chafe, *Never Stop Running: Allard Lowenstein and the Struggle to Save American Liberalism* (New York: Basic Books, 1993); on Kaufman, see Kevin Mattson, *Intellectuals in Action: The Origins of the New Left and Radical Liberalism, 1945–1970* (University Park, Penn State Press, 2002), chapter five.

5. See, especially here, the passages about Tom Hayden's interest in guerrilla warfare in James Miller, *Democracy Is in the Streets: From Port Huron to the Siege of Chicago* (New York: Simon and Schuster, 1987), pp. 273–76.

6. Todd Gitlin, *The Sixties: Years of Hope, Days of Rage* (New York: Bantam, 1987), p. 349.

7. See Rick Perlstein, *Before the Storm: Barry Goldwater and the Unmaking of the American Consensus* (New York: Hill and Wang, 2001).

8. Quoted in Perlstein, *Before the Storm,* p. 473.

9. Kenneth Heineman, *Put Your Bodies Upon the Wheels: Student Revolt in the 1960s* (Chicago: Ivan R. Dee, 2001), p. 75.

10. Heineman, *Put Your Bodies Upon the Wheels,* p. 208.

11. See Mattson, *Intellectuals in Action.*

CHAPTER 3

1. The words of these young people struck me as very similar to those of the "Angry Young Men" of Britain who complained about a lack of "big causes" during the 1950s (in comparison with the Old Left that came before).

2. Frank Ahrens, "For Activists Today, It's Marks, Not Marx," *Washington Post,* April 20, 2001, p. A10.

3. Jennifer Baumgardner and Amy Richards, *Manifesta: Young Women, Feminism, and the Future* (New York: Farrar, Straus and Giroux, 2000), pp. 21, 37.

4. See Robert Dreyfuss, "Till Earth and Heaven Ring: The NAACP Is Back, and It Plans on Being Heard," *The Nation*, July 23/30, 2001, p. 15.

5. Thomas Frank, *The Conquest of Cool* (Chicago: University of Chicago Press, 1998).

6. Juliet Schor, *The Overworked American: The Unexpected Decline of Leisure* (New York: Basic Books, 1991), pp. 26–27.

7. Daniel Pink, *Free Agent Nation: How America's New Independent Workers are Transforming the Way We Live* (New York: Warner Books, 2001), p. 254.

8. See Schor, *The Overworked American*, for more on these points.

9. John Judis, *The Paradox of American Democracy: Elites, Special Interests, and the Betrayal of the Public Trust* (New York: Pantheon, 2000), pp. 119, 134.

10. Thomas Frank, *One Market Under God: Extreme Capitalism, Market Populism, and the End of Economic Democracy* (New York: Doubleday, 2000), pp. 235, 245, 260.

11. Naomi Klein, *No Logo: Taking Aim at the Brand Bullies* (New York: Picador, 1999), p. 247.

12. Pink, *Free Agent Nation*, p. 203.

13. Quoted in Klein, *No Logo*, p. 268.

14. Sidney Verba, Kay Lehman Schlozman, and Henry Brady, *Voice and Equality: Civic Voluntarism in American Politics* (Cambridge: Harvard University Press, 1995), pp. 420, 436.

15. Kenneth Heineman, *Put Your Bodies Upon the Wheels: Student Revolt in the 1960s* (Chicago: Ivan R. Dee, 2001), p. 62.

16. Russell Jacoby, *Dogmatic Wisdom: How the Culture Wars Divert Education and Distract America* (New York: Doubleday, 1994), p. 3; see also Alexander Astin, Kenneth Green, and William Korn, *The American Freshman: Twenty Year Trends, 1966–1985* (Los Angeles: Higher Education Research Institute, 1987).

17. Jennifer Washburn, "The Kept University," *Atlantic Monthly*, March 2000, pp. 51–52.

18. Jacoby, *Dogmatic Wisdom*, p. 10.

19. National Center for Educational Statistics, Table 327: Current-fund revenue of degree-granting institutions by source, 1980–81 to 1995–96: posted at http://www.NCES.ED.gov.

20. Patricia M. Scherschel, *Student Debt Levels Continues to Rise: Stafford Indebtedness, 1999 Updated,* USA Group, Inc available at www.luminafoundation.org/Publications/pdfs/DebtBurden.pdf.

21. Zachary Karabell, *What's College For?: The Struggle to Define Higher Education* (New York: Basic Books, 1998), p. 232.

22. See Washburn, "The Kept University."

23. A well-received article that discusses this is David Brooks, "The Organization Kid," *The Atlantic Monthly,* April 2001, pp. 40–54.

24. See, in general, Putnam, *Bowling Alone,* and Theda Skocpol, "Associations Without Members," *American Prospect,* July-August 1999, pp. 66–73.

25. "Reconnecting People and Politics," in *The New Majority: Toward a Popular Progressive Politics,* ed. Stanley Greenberg and Theda Skocpol (New Haven: Yale University Press, 1997), p. 160.

26. All of the activists I spoke with mentioned this problem. I should note that I personally had a similar experience with Citizen Action during the mid-1980s.

CHAPTER 4

1. Nina Eliasoph, *Avoiding Politics: How Americans Produce Apathy in Everyday Life* (Cambridge: Cambridge University Press, 1998).

2. For more on these general points, see Eric Alterman, *Sound and Fury: The Making of the Punditocracy* (Ithaca: Cornell University Press, 1999) and Jeffrey Scheuer, *The Sound Bite Society* (New York: Four Walls Eight Windows, 1999).

3. Richard Kahlenberg and Ruy Teixeira, "A Better Third Way," *The Nation,* March 5, 2001, p. 16.

4. Jon Cowan and Rob Nelson, *Revolution X* (New York: Penguin, 1994), p. 8.

5. Ibid., p. xx.

6. Ibid., p. 25.

7. See, among others, Heather McLeod, "The Sole of a Generation," *American Prospect,* Spring 1995, p. 93; Stuart Miller, "The Death of Lead or Leave," in Richard Thau and Jay Heflin, ed., *Generations Apart: Xers vs. Boomers vs. The Elderly* (Amherst: Prometheus, 1997).

8. All quotations come from an information packet provided to me by Third Millennium.

9. Meredith Bagby, *We've Got Issues: The Get Real, No B.S., Guilt-Free Guide to What Really Matters* (New York: Public Affairs, 2000), pp. 87, 88.

10. Meredith Bagby, *Rational Exuberance: The Influence of Generation X on the New American Economy* (New York: Dutton, 1998), pp. xii, 192.

11. Bagby, *We've Got Issues*, pp. 54, 55.

12. Tad Friend, "It's, You Know, About Opinions and Stuff," *New York Times Magazine*, June 15, 1997, p. 36.

13. Michele Mitchell, *A New Kind of Party Animal: How the Young Are Tearing Up the American Political Landscape* (New York: Simon and Schuster, 1998), p. 34.

14. Ibid., pp. 191–92.

15. NASS, "New Millennium Project," pp. 6–7; see also Tobi Walker, "Service and Politics: The Lost Connection," Report prepared for the Ford Foundation, May 30, 2000.

16. See Nina Eliasoph, *Avoiding Politics*, pp. 31–32 for an important treatment of this point.

17. Jane Addams, *Twenty Years at Hull House* (1910; reprint, New York: Signet, 1961), p. 219.

18. Kenneth Baer, *Reinventing Democrats: The Politics of Liberalism from Reagan to Clinton* (Lawrence: University Press of Kansas, 2000), p. 33.

19. For more on this, see John Judis, *The Paradox of American Democracy*, Chapter 10.

20. Richard Rothenberg, *The Neoliberals: Creating the New American Politics* (New York: Simon and Schuster, 1984), chapter 18.

21. Steven Waldman, *The Bill: How the Adventures of Clinton's National Service Bill Reveal What is Corrupt, Comic, Cynical—and Noble—About Washington* (New York: Viking, 1995), p. 4.

22. Ibid., p. 239.

23. Ibid., p. 11.

24. Ibid., p. 243.

25. Tobi Walker, "Service and Politics: The Lost Connection," p. 25.

26. For more on the President's Summit and the other initiatives discussed in this paragraph, see Kevin Mattson, "Doing Good, Looking Marvelous," *The Baffler*, #11, 1998.

27. See Kevin Mattson, "Did Punk Matter?: Analyzing the Practices of a Youth Subculture During the 1980s," *American Studies* 42 (2001): 69–97.

28. See Paul Loeb, *Generation at the Crossroads: Apathy and Action on the American Campus* (New Brunswick: Rutgers University Press, 1994), chapter 21.

29. See Russell Jacoby, *Dogmatic Wisdom: How the Culture Wars Divert Education and Distract America* (New York: Doubleday, 1994), and Todd

Gitlin, *The Twilight of Common Dreams: Why America Is Wracked by Culture Wars* (New York: Metropolitan, 1995).

30. Quoted in Marc Cooper, "The Boys and Girls of (Union) Summer," *The Nation*, August 12/19, 1996, p. 18. See also Margot Hornblower, "Labor's Youth Brigade," *Time*, July 15, 1996.

31. See Laureen Lazarovici, "Engaged, Outraged, the Next Rage: The New Student Activism," *America @ Work*, April 2000, pp. 12–15.

32. Liza Featherstone, "The Student Movement Comes of Age," p. 23.

33. Interview with Wylie Chen.

34. For more on this issue, see *Social Policy*, Summer 2000, a special issue edited by Kevin Mattson that focused on the academic labor movement.

35. For more on these points, see Naomi Klein, *No Logo*.

36. http://www.usasnet.org/who.index.shtml.

37. http://www.corporations.org/democracy/history.html.

38. Ibid.

39. Featherstone, "The Student Movement Comes of Age." For an excellent discussion about this tension, see the exchange between Jeffrey Isaac and Liza Featherstone in *Dissent*, Fall 2001.

40. Some of this has started in the Isaac-Featherstone debate just cited.

Chapter 5

1. Mary Jane Turner and Scott Richardson, "Civic/Citizenship Education and the Social Studies in the United States," Paper for the Close Up Foundation, no date, Circulated via the New Jersey Civic Education Consortium (Eagleton Institute, Rutgers University). This study covers more than forty state curricula.

2. For a negative take on this, see Richard Rothstein, "What Produces a Voter? Seemingly Not Civics Class," *New York Times*, July 11, 2001, p. B10; William Galston argued at the American Political Science Association's 2000 roundtable on civic education that there is proof that basic knowledge about the way government works does enhance democratic participation.

3. See, for instance, Syd Golston, "Kids Voting USA," *Social Education*, October 1996, pp. 344–48.

4. "First Ever Study of Youth Voter Mobilization Shows Success," posted at http://www.youthvote2000.org/events/viewnewsarticle.cfm?newsid=25.

5. Quoted in "Rock the Vote," *Time*, June 15, 1992, p. 24.

6. Michael Lewis, "The Herd of Independent Minds," *The New Republic*, June 3, 1996, p. 20.

7. Quoted in Cyndee Miller, "Promoting Voting: It's Goodwill—and Good Business Too," *Marketing News*, October 26, 1992, p. 1.

8. Rock the Vote has recently moved beyond simply getting out the vote. It mounted a new campaign with the title "I'm a Politician," a campaign that highlighted youth activists around the country. Though interesting, it is not clear what it has accomplished. It should also be noted that some experiential educators have experimented with "media education" whereby young people analyze advertising and popular culture for its pernicious qualities. This seems a healthy development in this context.

9. See, here, The Walt Whitman Center for the Culture and Politics of Democracy, "Measuring Citizenship Final Report," 1997.

10. Kevin Mattson and Margo Shea, "Building Citizens" (booklet funded by the Haas Foundation, published by the Walt Whitman Center, 1998); see also, Kevin Mattson, "Think About It," *Who Cares: A Toolkit for Social Change*, March/April 1998.

11. Joel Westheimer and Joseph Kahne, "What Kind of Citizen? The Politics of Educating for Democracy," forthcoming, *Harvard Education Review*.

12. I have reported these findings directly to the William Penn Foundation and published them in briefer form in "Can Americans Achieve Civic Equality?" *PEGS* 10, no. 1 (2001).

13. Tobi Walker, "Service and Politics," pp. 20–21.

14. From 1999 to 2000, I was on the Research Committee of the New Jersey Civic Education Consortium.

15. Interview with Eric Cole, March 9, 2001.

16. Interview with Wendy Ray, February 22, 2001; also an interview with Hans Riemer, Executive Director of the 2030 Center, February 3, 2001.

17. See, especially, Susan George, "How to Win the War of Ideas," *Dissent*, Summer 1997, pp. 47–53; see also my own, "Where Are the Young Left Intellectuals?" *Social Policy*, Spring 1999, pp. 53–58. I also rely on a very helpful but unpublished report by David Kallick for the Open Society Institute.

18. For a sense of how this limitation acts on young academics, see Paul Sabin, "Academe Subverts Young Scholars' Civic Orientation," *Chronicle of Higher Education*, February 8, 2002.

19. Ted Halstead, "A Politics for Generation X," p. 34.

20. Kaufman in "Draft Manifesto for the Coalition for an Open Convention," Kaufman Archives, Box One, Folder on Coalition for an Open

Convention; for Kaufman's argument against a progressive Third Party run, see Kaufman, "New Party or New Democratic Coalition," *Dissent*, Summer 1969, p. 13. I discuss Kaufman in chapter five of *Intellectuals in Action*. See also, Kevin Mattson, "Rereading *The Radical Liberal* Today," *Dissent*, Summer 2000, pp. 93–96.

CHAPTER 6

1. Andrei Cherny, *The Next Deal: The Future of Public Life in the Information Age* (New York: Basic Books, 2000), pp. 38–39, 46, 212. See also, in this context, Daniel Pink's remarks on "just in time" politics: *Free Agent Nation*, p. 298.

INDEX

About the Author

KEVIN MATTSON, associate professor of history and a faculty associate at the Contemporary History Institute at Ohio University (Athens, Ohio), is a former youth activist in the Washington, D.C., area. He served as the associate director of the Walt Whitman Center for the Culture and Politics of Democracy at Rutgers University from 1995 to 2000, overseeing research projects related to participatory democracy, including engaging young people in public service as a means of civic education. He also has consulted with numerous organizations. The author of *Creating a Democratic Public: The Struggle for Urban Participatory Democracy During the Progressive Era* and *Intellectuals in Action: The Origins of the New Left and Radical Liberalism, 1945–1970* as well as coeditor of *Democracy's Moment: Reforming the American Political System for the 21st Century* (a collection of essays on the rise of an academic labor movement that will be published in 2003), he has written for numerous magazines and journals, both academic and popular.